CONTENTS

THE LOCH NE

LOCH NESS IN SCOTLAND IS HUGE, 1,000 Ft DEEP IN PLACES, 24 MILES LONG AND OFTEN A MILE WIDE.

BUT IS IT HOME TO A HUGE MONSTER?

St. COLUMBA VISITED LOCH NESS IN 565 AD AND, SO THE STORY GOES ONE OF HIS COMPANIONS WAS ATTACKED BY A MONSTER.

GO BACK, FOUL MONSTER!

THANK THE LORD, COLUMBA. YOU'VE MADE IT TURN AWAY.

THIS WAS THE FIRST OF MANY 'SIGHTINGS'.

In the past, practical jokers have played tricks on Nessie-spotters. In 1977, two schoolboys fooled a cameraman into believing that he had captured the monster moving on film.

4

GREAT MYSTERIES

Edited by Caroline Clayton
and Damian Kelleher

Written by Robert Nicholson

TWO-CAN

GREAT MYSTERIES

Copyright © Two-Can Publishing Ltd 1994

This edition first published in Great Britain
in 1994 by Two-Can Publishing Ltd
346 Old Street
London EC1V 9NQ
in association with Scholastic Publications Ltd

Printed and bound in Hong Kong
2 4 6 8 10 9 7 5 3 1

A catalogue record for this book is available
from the British Library

ISBN: 1 85434 269 X

Design by Elizabeth Bell. Art directed by Catherine Page. Picture research by Debbie Dorman. Production by Lis Clegg.

Front Cover Illustrations: Oliver Frey. Front Cover Photographs: Fortean Picture Library.

Picture Credits:
Fortean Picture Library: p5, 8/9, 10 (Rene Dahinden), 19tr (PUFORG) cr (Philip Panton), br (Rene Dahinden), 24/25, Aerofilms p12/13, Britstock-Ifa/JAY p14, South American Pictures/Tony Morrison p16/17, Mary Evans p18/19c, 19tl&cl, 26t, 30b, Popperfoto p19bl, Griffith Institute/Ashmolean Museum p20, World Pictures p21t, Bridgeman Art Library/Giraudon p21b, Syndication Int p22, Ronald Grant Archive p23t, Ardea/Francois Gohier p27, Leeds University p30t, 31.

Illustrations:
Oliver Frey p4/5, 6/7, 9, 10, 15, 16/17, 28, Maureen & Gordon Gray p11, 29, John James p20/21, Barry Mitchell p22, 27, Chris West p23, Bernard Long p24, 26b, Woody p31. Lettering: John Aldritch.

SS MONSTER

The Loch Ness Monster is a huge creature that some people believe lives deep in Loch Ness, a lake in northern Scotland.

Hundreds claim to have seen the animal which is nicknamed 'Nessie'. The monster is said to measure up to nine metres in length. And it is thought to have flippers, one or two humps and a long, thin neck. Is Nessie a plesiosaur, a marine reptile believed to have become extinct with the dinosaurs about 65 million years ago?

In the 1930s a new road was built to the loch, giving more people access to its shores. After this, there were even more sightings of Nessie reported.

NESSIE OR NOT NESSIE?

In 1960, the BBC broadcast a programme about the Loch Ness Monster. Many people claimed that the footage shown on the programme proved that Nessie really did exist.

The Loch Ness Monster has been given the scientific name Nessiteras rhombopteryx so it can be protected by a British law that safeguards rare animals.

Once again, people flocked to the lake and soon afterwards, the Loch Ness Investigation Bureau (or LNIB) was set up. LNIB scientists went to Loch Ness with some sophisticated underwater equipment to try to solve the case once and for all. Investigations with sonar, a device that uses sound to detect underwater objects, have found that there are large, moving bodies in Loch Ness.

But experts can't agree on exactly what the findings prove, so the monster mystery goes on. Meanwhile, all over the world, tales abound of other mysterious monsters lurking in rivers, lakes and seas...

▶ In 1934 a national newspaper published one of the first photographs of Nessie. Experts now believe that this photo is probably just an otter shot in close-up

Loch Ness isn't the only place in the world with a monster mystery. In North America alone there are more than 100 lakes where all manner of mythical monsters have been spotted. Some of them resemble extinct dinosaurs and others look like strange, cross-bred creatures.

Others still are said to look like real animals, only much bigger. One, known as the Beast of 'Busco, is said to be a giant, fish-gobbling turtle which some eyewitnesses claim is the size of a pickup truck. The people of Churubusco, Indiana, where the monster lives, have nicknamed it Oscar!

MONSTER MYTHS

But where is the proof? Despite thousands of sightings, no-one has ever found the body of a dead monster or even the remains of its bones. Hundreds of photographs have been taken, yet none provides certain proof of a real-life monster.

THE MONSTER DETECTIVES

★ Cryptozoology is the scientific study of animals that are not recognised or accepted by other scientists. Cryptozoologists pick a particular animal and try to prove it exists by finding bones, taking pictures or even capturing a live example if they're lucky!

Many animals have only been discovered by scientists in the last 150 years. The coelacanth is a fish which was thought to have become extinct 60 or 70 million years ago (at the same time as dinosaurs). But in 1938 some African fishermen caught one in the Indian Ocean.

Since then, several others have been fished out of the sea and studied. Surely there may be more 'extinct' animals just waiting to be discovered?

A MONSTER
Check out where the mythical crea

▲ FREAKY FAMILY
A monster called Manipogo is said to live in Lake Manitoba in Canada. Local people claim to have seen monsters in the lake for hundreds of years. In 1960, three beasts were spotted together – a monster family of mother, father and baby!

NORTH AMERICA

NORTH ATLANTIC OCEAN

PACIFIC OCEAN

SOUTH AMERICA

▲ HE IS THE CHAMP!
In the depths of Lake Champlain, on the border of New York State and Canada, lurks a monstrous creature which is affectionately known as 'Champ'.

The lake is 168 kilometres (101 miles) long and over 100 metres deep – big enough for a monster to make its home. First spotted in 1609, Champ was finally photographed in 1977. He's said to be nearly 10 metres (33ft) long with the head of a huge horse. Neigh!

EUROPE

ASIA

AFRICA

PACIFIC
OCEAN

INDIAN
OCEAN

OUTH
TLANTIC
OCEAN

AUSTRALIA

▲ SQUIDS ALIVE!

In the 1930s, a 150,000-tonne tanker called the *Brunswick* was attacked by a giant squid. Eventually, the monster was chopped to pieces by the ship's propellers. Twenty-metre (66ft) specimens have been recorded in the past and some cryptozoologists claim that huge 50-60 metre (165-200ft) monster squid lurk deep in the tropical oceans.

◀ REWARD – $2,000!

Mokele-Mbembe is a large reptile said to live in the swamps of Central Africa. It was first reported some 200 years ago and takes its name from a word meaning 'he who stops the flow of rivers'. Could Mokele-Mbembe be a type of dinosaur that has survived from the Cretaceous era, 65 million years ago? There is a $2,000 reward for anyone who can produce evidence of its existence.

▲ SPOTTED!

Aboriginal people in Australia tell stories of a giant monster which they call Bunyip. In the early 19th century, an escaped convict called William Buckley claimed he saw one which was the size of a huge dog, complete with fins for swimming.

If you go down to the woods today, you're in for a big hairy surprise!

Big Hairy Monsters, or BHMs as they are called, have been sighted all over the world. From the west coast of the USA and Canada, through China, Mongolia, Russia and the Himalayas, there are thousands of eye-witness reports of hairy man-ape beasts. But what are these creatures? Can we prove they exist?

BHMs are usually between 1.5 and 2.5 metres tall (around five to eight feet), covered in thick black or reddish-brown hair. A typical BHM looks like a cross between a human being and an ape, or like a primitive human.

A BHM BY ANY OTHER NAME...

North America *Sasquatch* (native American name), *Big Foot*

Himalayas *Metoh-Kangmi* (Tibetan for Abominable Snowman), *Yeti* (Tibetan for Mountain Creature or Spirit)

China *Yeren*

Mongolia and Urals *Alma*

Australia *Yowie* (Aboriginal name)

HORRIBLE AND *Hairy!*

MONSTER MEETINGS

There's one thing all BHM witnesses are agreed upon. Almost everyone who has come close to one says the creatures are really smelly. So if you go on a Yeti hunt, don't forget the peg for your nose!

IN 1941 LIEUTENANT KARAPETYAN OF THE SOVIET ARMY WAS SHOWN A VERY STRANGE PRISONER.

IT MUST BE REAL, YOU CAN SEE IT FLINCH WHEN I PLUCK ITS HAIRS.

WAS THIS CREATURE ALSO A YETI? IT ESCAPED, SO NO-ONE KNEW FOR SURE.

IN 1979 A SHERPA FRIGHTENED AWAY A YETI WITH A STICK...

GET OUT OF HERE, YOU HORRIBLE CREATURE.

LATER FRENCH SCIENTISTS EXAMINED SOME HAIRS FROM THE END OF THE STICK — AND DISCOVERED THEY CAME FROM AN **UNKNOWN** PRIMATE!

THOUSANDS OF BIGFOOT SIGHTINGS HAVE BEEN REPORTED BUT MANY ARE HOAXES...

YOU TERRIFIED PEOPLE WITH YOUR BIGFOOT COSTUME. I'M FINING YOU $100.

▲ In 1967, ace monster-tracker Roger Patterson managed to film a Big Foot. These are still photos from his cine-film. Scientific experts who analysed the film were astounded and could not decide whether it showed a real BHM or a tall man in a hairy suit.

"I couldn't see the zipper, and I still can't," said John Napier of the Smithsonian Institute, a scientific research college in the United States.

FOOT NOTES

Do the huge footprint photos prove that the incredible Yeti really does exist?

THE CAMERA NEVER LIES!

IN 1951 ERIC SHIPTON, A BRITISH MOUNTAINEER, ARRIVED BACK FROM THE HIMALAYAS.

I HAVE SOME AMAZING PICTURES HERE OF HUGE, STRANGE FOOTPRINTS.

DID SHIPTON HAVE THE EVIDENCE THAT PROVED THE EXISTENCE OF YETIS?

★ Or does it? Some BHM tracks have been photographed in America and in the Himalayas. They seem to indicate that the BHM prints are nothing like an ape's. For a start, apes' feet have a thumb, which is certainly not visible in BHM tracks. Photographs of BHMs and their footprints can be misleading. The repeated melting and freezing of prints left in snow can greatly alter their shape and size. Many photos of BHMs are blurred and very faint. And some have been proved to be positive fakes.

▲ This is one of the pictures that Eric Shipton took on his 1951 expedition. It sparked off scores of Yeti hunts in the Himalayas

YETI OR BIGFOOT. WHATEVER YOU CALL IT, DOES IT EXIST?

UGH! URGH!

LAND OF THE GIANTS

★ Other theories suggest that they are survivors of the species *Giantopithecus*. This was a giant ape which lived in China and was thought to have become extinct 300,000 years ago. Giantopithecus could have crossed the Bering Strait into America, exactly as the American Indians and Eskimos did, around 12,000 years ago.

THREE-SIDED MYSTERY
The Bermuda Triangle covers an area of roughly 1,140,000 square kilometres. That's some triangle!

VANISHING POINT

What terrible secret lies within the Bermuda Triangle?

Off the south-east coast of America, there lies an area of the Atlantic Ocean known as the Bermuda Triangle. Within this zone, more than 50 ships and planes have disappeared in mysterious circumstances this century. What's especially puzzling is that few captains or pilots have sent radio distress messages before they vanished forever.

The first recorded disappearance took place in 1918 when USS *Cyclops* vanished while sailing through the area. Then in 1945, a squadron of five US bomber planes disappeared without trace near the Bahamas. The US navy sent out a search plane to investigate but that, too, failed to return.

OUT OF FUEL, OUT OF LUCK?

What could have happened to the missing planes? All the pilots in the squadron were trainees, and it's possible that they simply lost their way and ran out of fuel. As for the search plane, some witnesses claim to have seen an explosion over the area. This could have been the plane blowing up – after all, this particular aircraft was known by pilots as 'the Flying Gas Tank'.

NEW-FANGLED ANGLE

In 1964, a journalist called Vincent Gaddis published a book about the area. This was the first time that the phrase 'Bermuda Triangle' was used and it created a huge stir. Soon, accounts of other disappearances within the area came flooding in – as they still do today.

WHAT'S GOING ON?

⭐ Nobody knows for sure what causes these strange disappearances. Some scientists claim that sudden shifts in the Earth's magnetic field in the area may be to blame. Or perhaps downward air currents are the key to the mystery. And some even believe that UFOs and aliens are the cause of all the problems. Beam me up, Scotty!

MONUMEN

TAL MYSTERY

There's nothing plain about the stunning Stone Age spectacle in Wiltshire

Two hundred years before the Egyptians built the Great Pyramid, Stone Age Britons began work on a huge circle of rocks. But just why is still a mystery.

Stone circles were built in Europe from about 3000 to 1200 BC. There are more than 900 in Britain alone and Stonehenge, on Salisbury Plain in Wiltshire, is perhaps the greatest of them all.

MUSCLE MEN

Its construction is a brain-boggling feat. Stonehenge was built with pure muscle power – the Stone Age Britons who built it had no iron tools for digging and carving. And at that time, they didn't even have the wheel to help them drag the huge stones along.

Hundreds of men would have toiled long and hard to create Britain's best-known prehistoric monument. The upright stones (called sarsens) in the outer circle came from the Marlborough Downs, over 30 kilometres (18 miles) away. And it's thought that the bluestones standing upright in the inner circle came from Pembrokeshire in Wales. That's over 200 kilometres (120 miles) away! Imagine the effort of dragging stones weighing up to four tonnes each over sea and land. More than 600 men would have been needed to pull each stone!

In 1988, a bluestone was found on the bed of the River Daugleddau at Llsngwm in Wales. It is a similar size and shape to those of Stonehenge and experts believe it fell off its raft during the journey.

SECRET OF THE STONES

But the real mystery of the monument is its purpose. What was it used for? It might have been a religious centre where ceremonies were held and sacrifices made. Some experts believe it was some kind of astronomical observatory used for studying the sun, moon and stars.

Whatever the answer, it must have been important to the ancient people who built it. After all, researchers estimate it would have taken millions of hours and hundreds of years to complete.

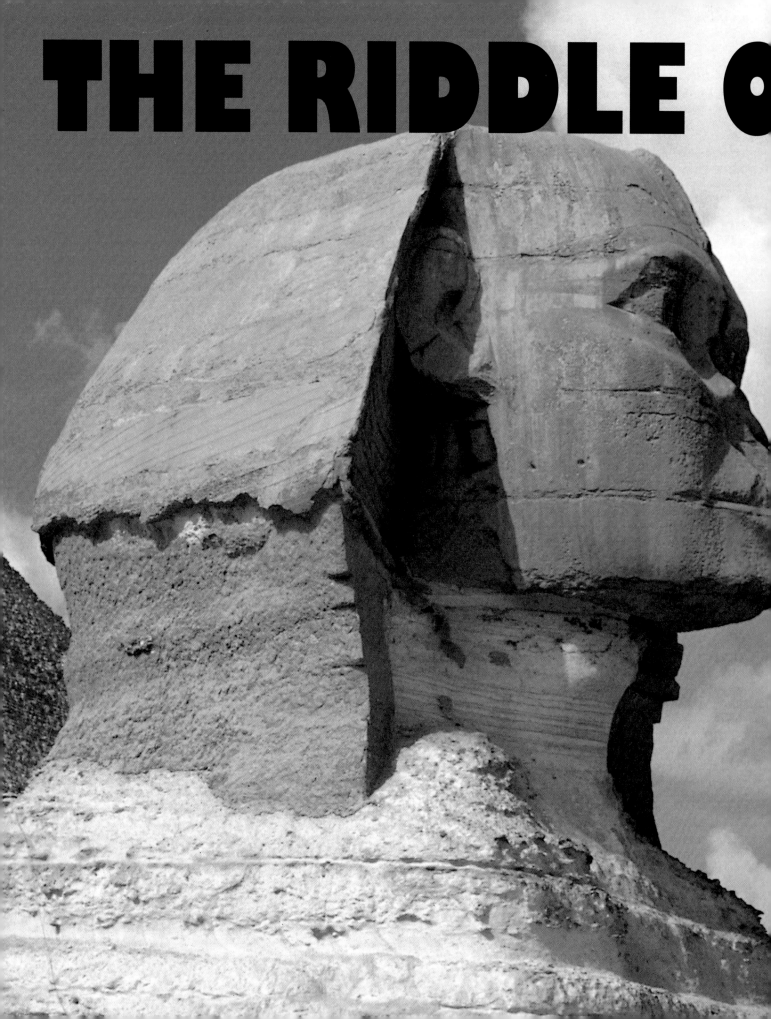

THE SPHINX

Can you solve the puzzle behind the guardian of the pyramids?

At Giza, in Egypt, a strange statue stands guard over the tombs of the Pharaohs. With the head of a human and the body of a lion, the fearsome beast was meant to keep robbers away from the precious pyramids.

STONE ME!

It's hard to believe that the incredible sphinx was built about 4,500 years ago. The whole of the impressive statue at Giza, except for its legs and paws, is carved from one single piece of rock. At this time, the Egyptians often sculpted sphinxes to honour a king or queen.

In full, it measures 20 metres (66ft) high, 73 metres (240ft) long and its face is over four metres (13ft) wide. The face was modelled on Khafre, one of the Pharaohs of Egypt.

RIDDLE-ME-RI

The sphinx is found in many cultures, though – not just in that of ancient Egypt. In Greek mythology, for example, it has the body of a lion, the head of a woman, a pair of wings and a serpent's tail. According to Greek legend, the sphinx asked everyone who saw her a riddle. The punishment for getting the answer wrong was instant death!

"What animal, with only one voice, has four feet in the morning, two feet at midday, and three feet at sunset?" Can you work it out for yourself?

PROBLEM SOLVED

Finally, a Greek prince called Oedipus gave the sphinx the correct answer. It was "a man". When first he is a baby, man crawls on all fours. Then as he grows, he walks on two legs, and finally, as an old man, leans on a stick – the 'third foot' of the riddle.

The sphinx was so furious that someone had finally solved her riddle that she jumped off the high rock she lived on – to her death.

WHAT A BEAST!

A round-up of some other creepy mythical creatures – part human, part animal

Griffin
Griffins (above) had the head and wings of an eagle, the body of a lion and the tail of a snake. They were very greedy and loved feasting upon people and horses!

Unicorn
The unicorn was like a horse with a single horn in the middle of its head. It was probably based on the rhinoceros.

Centaur
Centaurs had a horse's body and the head and shoulders of a man. They loved whooping it up and spent most of their time getting drunk. Hic!

Minotaur
This infamous monster (below) lived in the labyrinth below the palace of King Minos of Crete. Part bull and part man, the beast was fed seven maidens and seven youths every nine years, until Theseus of Athens finally killed it in an epic struggle.

Back in the 16th century, when Spanish explorers first arrived in South America, there was talk of a fabulously rich native Indian king called El Dorado – the Golden Man.

He was said to live in a beautiful city, hidden deep in the jungle, where the streets were paved with gold.

PRECIOUS DUST

Legend had it that once a year a ceremony was held to show the power and wealth of the king. He was covered in clay and then sprinkled all over with gold dust. Amidst music and singing he was taken to the centre of a lake on a raft, where he dived in and then emerged, the gold now washed off and sinking to the bottom.

Explorers from Europe flocked to what is now Columbia to find the lake, the city and the gold. For centuries, prospectors have searched for the legendary golden city of El Dorado, but still it remains undiscovered.

THE GOLDEN LAKE

Lake Guatavita, in Colombia, sits 2,300 metres (9,000ft) above sea-level in the crater of an extinct volcano. In 1540, Spanish treasure-seeker Hernán Perez de Quesada spent three unsuccessful

▲ Is the legend of El Dorado – the Golden Man – true?

months trying to drain the lake dry. He believed this was where El Dorado had bathed – and left his gold behind!

Another attempt to drain the lake began in 1580, but only one emerald and a few gold trinkets were found by the Colombian

merchant behind this ill-fated venture. Then, in 1912, the lake was drained completely, revealing precious little gold. What was removed was valued at roughly one tenth of the cost of the whole project – certainly not worth the effort!

LOST CITY

What became of El Dorado, the legendary golden city of South America?

▲ Is Lake Guatavi

...den wonder? It seems not!

▲ *Could the city of Atlantis have looked like this?*

LOST AND FOUND

★ Legend has it that thousands of years ago, there was a wealthy and highly advanced civilisation on an island called Atlantis. Volcanic eruptions destroyed the city and it sank beneath a massive tidal wave – lost forever.

Earlier this century, an American psychic called Edgar Cayce claimed he had visited Atlantis in a trance. He said its people had developed X-rays and televisions and he pinpointed Bimini, in the Bahamas, as the site. He also predicted that part of the city would be revealed in 1968. Amazingly, two divers did discover huge parallel lines of stones under the sea off the coast of Bimini that very year. Was this the lost city of Atlantis?

TROJAN TROVE
For hundreds of years, the city of Troy was considered nothing more than a legend. Then, in 1873, a German archaeologist called Heinrich Schliemann discovered the city walls in northern Turkey and proved its existence. Maybe it won't be long before experts find conclusive proof of Atlantis's existence too, and the history books will have to be rewritten.

UFOS

No, it isn't a bird and it isn't a plane. So what are the strange shapes that have been spotted in our skies?

Unidentified Flying Objects (UFOs) first hit the headlines way back in 1947.

Businessman Kenneth Arnold was flying over the Cascade Mountains in the USA when he saw what looked like nine circular, metallic objects. They were flying in formation at great speed, weaving in and out of the mountain peaks. They didn't look like planes and Arnold described them as "a chain of saucer-like things".

Soon reports of 'flying saucers' were flooding in from all over the world. Now, nearly 50 years on, an average of about 40 sightings are reported every day.

BALLS OF CONFUSION

So what exactly is a UFO? Without a doubt, some of the sightings are hoaxes. Then again, some are probably illusions created by atmospheric conditions – cloud formations or ball lightning – while others may be high-altitude weather balloons or satellites breaking up on re-entry to the atmosphere.

But that still leaves other sightings which can't be explained away as simply. Could these be visits by alien beings from outer space? Check out these reported sightings and decide for yourself!

● The cigar-shaped UFO that a jazz band saw in Glasgow in 1955 fits the exact description of one that visited Manchester in 1982. Did the UFO come back for a second look at our planet?

● US Air Force pilot Thomas Mantell saw a huge, metallic UFO in 1948. He chased it high into the sky before his own plane came crashing inexplicably back down to earth.

TOO CLOSE FOR COMFORT

UFOlogists divide UFO incidents into three kinds of close encounter:

1 Close encounters of the first kind (CE1) are classed as UFO sightings.

2 Close encounters of the second kind (CE2) are sightings and permanent evidence, such as marks in the ground or burns on grass.

3 Close encounters of the third kind (CE3) – that's contact with alien beings from a UFO.

▲ *Saucers over Sicily: several witnesses spotted these UFOs back in 1954*

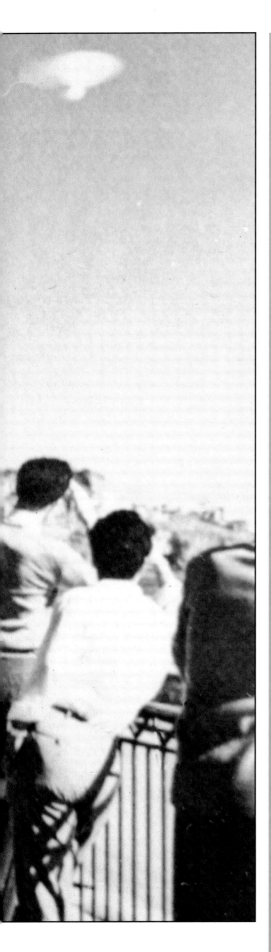

PROOF POSITIVE?

These photos are 'evidence' of famous UFO sightings. But are they real or fake? It's up to you to decide!

▲This flying saucer zoomed into Paul Trent's viewfinder one evening in Oregon, USA

▲ Ignore the giraffe – what's that strange object to the left? Just another tall story, perhaps?!

▲ These discs put several quarry workers in a quandary in Larchant, France

▲ It came from anywhere but outer space. These spheres are definite fakes!

▲ Looks like a lampshade? Well it's Adamski's flying saucer, photographed back in 1952

▲ Cosmic clouds at Mount Shasta – or visitors from another planet?

WHOOPS!
The planet Venus is called 'the Queen of the UFOs' because it's been mistaken for one so many times!

Did a dreadful fate await the discoverers of King Tut's tomb?

In 1917, an English archaeologist called Howard Carter began excavations in the Valley of the Kings. His aim was to find the tomb of the boy king, Tutankhamun, who died in 1339 BC when he was just 18.

Carter's search was funded by Lord Caernarvon, a wealthy aristocrat. But by 1922, money was running out and it looked as though the whole quest would have to be called off.

HIDDEN ENTRANCE

Then, on 26 November 1922, Carter and Caernarvon discovered the entrance to Tutankhamun's tomb. It had been hidden under debris thrown up by a dig at another tomb in the valley.

Egyptian workers helping Carter and Caernarvon were very superstitious about the discovery. They believed that the lucky pair had found the tomb largely thanks to the pet canary that Howard Carter had bought recently.

Shortly after the discovery, James Brested, an American archaeologist, heard a loud "almost human" cry from behind Carter's quarters. The canary had been killed by a king cobra, a creature that was often used to represent Tutankhamun himself.

Immediately, there was talk of a curse on the tomb, and terrible fates that would befall those who had opened it up.

Within weeks, Lord Caernarvon was dead after an insect bite became infected. He was just 53. At the very moment when he died, all the lights in Cairo went out for no reason at all. Back home, his trusty dog let out a terrible howl and collapsed – dead.

GET CARTER

Two more victims of the 'curse' followed shortly afterwards. George Bendite, an archaeologist and Arthur Mace, a friend of Carter, both died suddenly after visiting the site. By now, rumours of a curse were spreading fast.

Yet the one person who remained untouched by the curse was Carter himself.

He spent a further 10 years clearing and cataloguing the contents of the amazing tomb – a considerable task. Eventually, he died of natural causes in 1939.

CURSE CONTINUES

In 1962, Dr Ezzedin Taha thought he had solved the mystery of Tutankhamun's dreaded curse once and for all. He claimed the numerous deaths that had followed the opening of the tomb could all be traced back to one cause – deadly bacteria.

Dr Taha's theory stated that dangerous, disease-carrying bacteria had been sealed into the tomb along with the boy king and his glittering prizes. So when the tomb was reopened, its innocent discoverers walked straight into a fatal trap.

Alas, Dr Taha never had the chance to conduct further research to prove his theory. Just days after explaining away the catastrophic curse to the world, he too died – in a mysterious car crash.

▲ 3,000 years old and still a mummy's boy!

FIND OF THE CENTURY

▲ *This solid gold mask showing the young king's face covered the head and shoulders of Tutankhamun's mummy. It is thought to show him as the sun-god*

THIS IS MADE FROM SOLID GOLD!

AND EVERYTHING IS PERFECTLY PRESERVED!

★ Howard Carter (left) and Lord Caernarvon (right) are the names behind the most exciting archaeological discovery this century.

"Can you see anything?" Caernarvon asked Carter. "Yes, wonderful things!" Carter replied. And he was right. Inside the tomb were all manner of beautiful items including trumpets, thrones and several statues of the boy king himself.

Most other pharaohs' tombs had been plundered by robbers hundreds of years before. But apart from a side room which had been disturbed, Tutankhamun's treasures were found exactly as they had been left more than 32 centuries before!

EGYPTIAN AFTERLIFE

The Egyptians were firm believers in life after death. To prepare them for the next world, they mummified (embalmed and dried) corpses to prevent the bodies from decaying. People were usually buried with their favourite possessions and objects that would be of practical use to them in the afterlife.

The Egyptians also believed that jewellery was a lucky charm against danger. Favourite pieces like this scarab brooch (below) found in Tut's chamber were placed with them in the tombs but some were also specially made to fit the mummy.

At the funeral, a priest would touch the mummy's mouth, hands and feet so that the spirit could enter the body in the afterlife. Then it was ready to breathe again.

MIND OVER MATTER

Is Uri Geller the greatest modern magician or a mind-bending psychic?

URI GELLER'S POWERS WERE WITH HIM FROM AN EARLY AGE.

HOW ON EARTH DID YOU BEND THAT SPOON, URI?

I JUST GAVE IT A RUB, GRANDMA-HONEST!

BY 1969, URI WAS SHOWING OFF HIS AMAZING SKILLS TO THE PUBLIC...

THAT'S IMPOSSIBLE! YOU CAN'T BEND A KEY WITH YOUR FINGER-TIPS.

JUST WATCH. I'LL SHOW YOU.

SOON URI'S SPOON-BENDING WAS FAMOUS ALL OVER THE WORLD.

MY WATCH... IT'S STARTED UP AGAIN.

GELLERMANIA

BUT THAT OLD THING'S BEEN BROKEN FOR YEARS!

SCIENTISTS WERE DETERMINED TO PROVE URI WAS A FRAUD.

HE MUST BE A MAGICIAN!

HE CAN'T BE DOING IT WITH THE POWER OF HIS MIND!

BUT MANY OTHERS DID BELIEVE HIM...

SO YOU'LL HELP US FIND OIL, URI? WE'LL PAY YOU WELL.

YES! I'M SURE THERE'S OIL HERE SOMEWHERE...

I CAN FEEL IT!

BY 1985, WHEN HE CAME TO LIVE IN BRITAIN, HE WAS A MILLIONAIRE.

Uri Geller has bent forks and spoons, fixed broken watches and read people's minds all over the world.

Born in Tel Aviv in 1946, he first appeared on British television on 23 November 1973, when he bent a fork by stroking it gently with his fingers. Hundreds of people called the BBC to say that they too had bent forks whilst watching him. Gellermania swept the country.

Some sceptics claimed that he used force, so a device to measure pressure was rigged up to the brass strip he was rubbing. It showed just 15 grams of pressure – not nearly enough to bend metal.

TRICK OR TREAT

Experts at the Stanford Research Institute in California could find no trace of fakery or trickery. However, a magician called James Randi has fooled scientists by bending cutlery using magic tricks.

Is Uri Geller the cleverest magician ever or does he really have incredible psychic powers? A number of scientists have tried to show that he is a fake, but no-one has ever been able to prove it.

▲ Uri doesn't use force to bend steel spoons – he just strokes them gently

Are these amazing winged relatives of the dinosaurs still alive and well?

Eighty million years ago, the pterosaur ruled the airways! Undisputed king of the skies, this massive, flying reptile had a wing span of up to 11 metres (36ft). Although it is thought that the pterosaur died out with the rest of its dino cousins, there have been reports of similar, winged beasts sighted in recent times.

In 1933, two British Museum scientists saw a giant, bat-like creature flying over a river in Cameroon. As large as a huge eagle, local tribesmen called it an Olitiau. Similar creatures have also been seen in Zimbabwe, Namibia, Zambia and the Sierra Madre mountains in Mexico.

BATTY BIRD

In Java, legends abound of the Athol, a giant fur-covered, bat-like bird with the face of a monkey. The creature is said to be named after its long, howling call (aah-ooool). Those who have seen the Athol all talk of its weird turned-back feet. Dr Ernest Bartels, who has himself spotted the Athol, is convinced it is actually a species of giant bat, rather than a survivor of the dinosaur era. After all, bats' feet do point backwards – and their funny-looking faces are quite similar to those of monkeys.

If the pterosaur has survived from the age of the dinosaurs, it does raise some very important questions. For a start, how could such a massive creature hide itself away for so long? And how on earth did it manage to survive throughout the centuries?

▲ *Pterosaurs dominated the skies for almost as long as dinosaurs ruled the earth*

LIVING LEGENDS

SWOOP SCOOP

★ The thunderbird is a giant bird in native American mythology, based on a condor or eagle. In 1886, hunters killed an enormous bird and measured its wingspan. Six men, standing fingertip to fingertip, could only just stretch from the tip of one wing to the other – a distance of about 10 metres (33ft)!

A plane that crashed in Maryland, USA in 1962 was found to be covered in blood and birds' feathers. Officials said it had flown into a flock of geese. But could geese have made the huge gouge marks on its fuselage? Or was it brought down by a giant thunderbird?

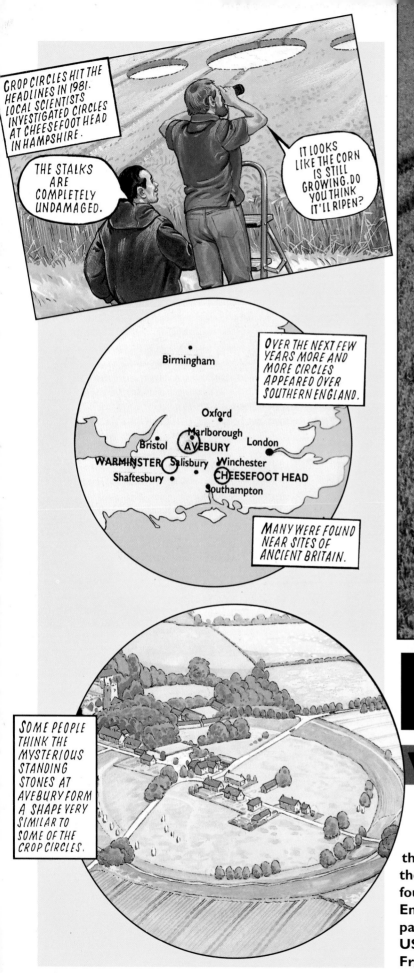

CROP CIRCLES HIT THE HEADLINES IN 1981. LOCAL SCIENTISTS INVESTIGATED CIRCLES AT CHEESEFOOT HEAD IN HAMPSHIRE.

THE STALKS ARE COMPLETELY UNDAMAGED.

IT LOOKS LIKE THE CORN IS STILL GROWING. DO YOU THINK IT'LL RIPEN?

OVER THE NEXT FEW YEARS MORE AND MORE CIRCLES APPEARED OVER SOUTHERN ENGLAND.

Birmingham

Oxford

Marlborough

AVEBURY

London

Bristol

WARMINSTER Salisbury Winchester

Shaftesbury CHEESEFOOT HEAD

Southampton

MANY WERE FOUND NEAR SITES OF ANCIENT BRITAIN.

SOME PEOPLE THINK THE MYSTERIOUS STANDING STONES AT AVEBURY FORM A SHAPE VERY SIMILAR TO SOME OF THE CROP CIRCLES.

MAGIC

What makes these strange

Crop circles were first officially recorded back in the 19th century. Since then, several have been found all over southern England and in other parts of the world – the USA, Brazil, Australia, France and Russia.

They are often formed in fantastic and beautiful shapes. Circles make up the basic pattern but there have also been ringed circles, spoked wheels, rectangles and straight lines. More complex pictograms have also been found in the shape of dolphins, stars or even

CIRCLES

wirling patterns in the countryside?

★ In July 1990, one of the most wonderful crop configurations ever appeared at Alton Barnes in the Vale of Pewsey, Wiltshire.

Over 80 metres long, this was the first in a series of 'double pictograms' and boasted ringed circles with 'satellites' at the top of the formation. These circles have distinctive 'lock' shapes, which almost seemed to suggest that someone (or something) was trying to provide the key to the mystery. But what was it?

Fake or genuine, the Alton Barnes circles proved to be big business. Thousands of people flocked to inspect the pattern at close quarters and the canny farmer who owned the field made himself a profit by charging visitors an entrance fee!

letters of the alphabet.

One of the most complex pictograms to date was found in August 1991. It formed the shape of a mathematical pattern called a Mandelbrot Set, which is known only to scientists, mathematicians, computer buffs... and possibly intelligent aliens or very clever hoaxers!

HOW CIRCLES APPEAR
The crop is usually flattened in delicately-layered swirls, each stalk bent to the ground without killing the plant. Scientists have examined seeds and plants taken from circles and found that they have altered cell structures and are often malformed in strange ways. Yet the scientists seem unable to explain how these very unusual changes occur.

Are the crop circles just clever hoaxes? Turn over and find out.

THE HOAXES

Are the mysterious circles simply the work of petty pranksters?

In the summer of 1991, British hoaxers Doug Brewer and Dave Chorley made an astonishing claim. They announced that they were responsible for many of the crop circles that had baffled top scientists.

Newspapers and TV crews gathered to interview the two pranksters, confident that the 'mystery' had finally been solved. But soon, some important questions began to arise. Could two elderly men really have created hundreds of circles all over the country? How did they manage to move around at night without being seen by anyone? And just how did they get into the middle of fields without leaving tracks?

PUT THE BOOT IN

Another group of hoaxers, calling themselves the Wessex Sceptics, also declared that they were responsible for many of the strange crop circles.

Hoaxers claim that the shapes are made by using planks of wood attached to lengths of string or chains, wound around a central pole. Some even reckon that the best way is to trample the crop down in a circular shape with nothing more sophisticated than a pair of hefty boots! But none of these methods would have created the beautiful curled, swirled and layered patterns that the flattened stalks usually leave behind.

WHODUNNIT?

Crop circle experts claim that they can always tell which of the circles are faked – most fakes are more ragged, with lots of broken plant stalks. And farmers usually know when strangers have been walking in their fields. Could the hoaxers really have got away with it?

In the USA, a huge crop pattern at Highland, Kansas was claimed to be a prank. But someone was taking it seriously – the mysterious government 'investigators' who sealed off the area, tried to hide the circle and prevented the item from appearing on the local news.

In Grasdorf, Germany a huge 600-square-metre pattern was claimed to be a hoax. But such a vast and precisely-detailed example would be difficult to achieve without the hoaxers attracting attention.

Some experts on crop circles believe that small whirlpools of air could cause the shapes. But would they be able to make some of the fine detailing seen in so many of these strange phenomena? Or is it possible that crop circles are special signs left behind by visitors from outer space – coded messages that we haven't yet learned to crack?

TALK OF THE DEVIL

★ Crop circles became big news in the 1990s but it looks as though there may be nothing new about these fascinating field phenomena.

Wood carvings dating back to the late 17th century have been found which seem to show the devil cutting down crops in a circular shape. And later images such as this one, below, show a horned devil being shooed away from 'his work' – possibly a crop circle – by a female fieldworker.

But are these images concrete evidence of devilish crop circle connections? It doesn't seem likely – after all, the devil often features strongly in country superstitions and usually takes the blame for anything which can't be readily explained!

IN 1991 DAVE CHORLEY AND DOUG BREWER CLAIMED THEY HAD MADE THE CIRCLES.

IT'S ALL A BIG JOKE – WE MADE THE CIRCLES.

AND LOTS OF PEOPLE HAVE BEEN COPYING US.

EXPERTS GATHERED TO CHECK THEIR STORY...

YOU DO IT LIKE THIS, WITH BOARDS AND STRING. WE'VE BEEN DOING IT FOR YEARS!

BUT YOU'RE BREAKING THE STALKS – THAT'S MUCH MORE RAGGED THAN A REAL CIRCLE.

ARE THEY MAD BY HOAXERS OR BY FREAK WEATHER CONDITIONS?

OR IS IT A MYSTER ENERGY – MAYBE AN ALIEN SPACEC YOU DECIDE!

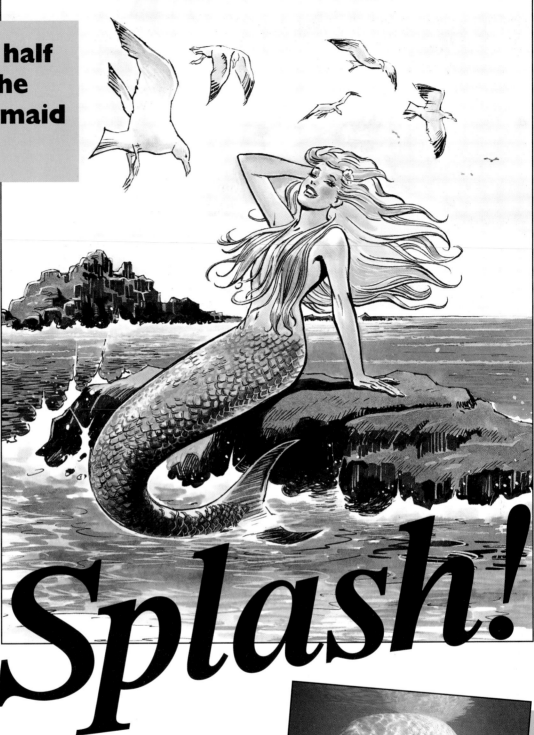

Half woman, half fish – but is the amazing mermaid just a myth?

Folk tales from all over the world tell of a race of creatures, half human, half fish, that live at the bottom of the sea. But are these stories just fishy tales?

From head to waist, legend has it that merfolk look just like ordinary humans. But from the waist down, they're said to be covered in scales. Most folklore focuses on the females, mythical maids who sit on rocks, combing their long, golden hair and admiring themselves in their mirrors. A couple of centuries ago, every sailor was warned of these malicious sirens who would sing sweetly to passing sailors, luring them to their doom on dangerous rocks.

MER-MANIA!

Columbus reported seeing three mermaids on his voyage to America in 1492. But many sightings have also taken place on the Scottish coast. In 1833, six Shetland fishermen apparently caught a mermaid in their nets off the island of Yell. For three hours she howled miserably, until they released her into the sea.

Just three years earlier, in 1830, another mermaid was found off the west coast of Scotland, on the island of Benbecula. Locals cutting seaweed had spotted her frolicking in the sea a few days earlier, before her body was washed up on the beach. So sure was the local sheriff that she was at least part human that he ordered a shroud and coffin for the poor, beautiful creature.

MISTAKEN IDENTITY

Nowadays, few modern scientists take the mermaid theory seriously. It's widely believed that the manatee, the dugong, or even dolphins, could have been mistaken for mermaids by lonely sailors. Sounds as though they'd been away from their wives for too long!

▲ *What a mix-up! Would you confuse a manatee with a mermaid?*

THE FLYING DUTCHMAN

The ghostly galleon that takes to the high seas on a never-ending voyage

It is March 1939. The beach at False Bay, near Cape Town, is packed with sunbathers and swimmers. It is a bright, sunny day and suddenly a huge sailing ship is spotted in the bay. It's under full sail, yet there's not a breath of wind. How can this be?

Over 100 people witnessed the appearance of this ship. Minutes later it vanished. Could this have been the notorious ghostly galleon, the *Flying Dutchman*, said to be cursed to sail the seven seas until the end of time?

The legend began with Hendrik van der Decken, the Dutch skipper of a ship sailing from Holland to the East Indies. The *Flying Dutchman* hit a bad storm around the Cape of Good Hope and the crew begged van der Decken to turn back. He refused, swearing he would round the Cape "or be forever damned". When the vessel finally lost its battle against the elements, van der Decken was doomed to sail his ship until the end of time.

CELEBRITY SPOTTER

Hundreds of sailors claim to have seen the ghost ship. Prince George, later King George V of Britain, was a midshipman on HMS *Inconstant*. On 11 July 1881, he saw the *Flying Dutchman* off the coast of Australia. Thirteen others in the crew also saw the ship. Rumour and superstition surround most sightings, and this one is no exception. Shortly after the ghost ship's appearance, the very first sailor who caught sight of it dropped dead.

MAYDAY! MAYDAY! Today, sailors believe that an appearance by the *Flying Dutchman* is a sure sign of approaching danger.

THE MYSTERY OF THE MARY CELESTE

LOOK AT THAT STRANGE SHIP, SIR. SHE'S SAILING VERY BADLY.

ON 5 DECEMBER 1872, THE CREW OF A BRITISH VESSEL, THE **DEI GRATIA**, CAME ACROSS A STRANGE SHIP DRIFTING IN THE ATLANTIC...

When a ship called the *Mary Celeste* was found abandoned in 1872, the discovery raised many intriguing questions. For a start, there was no sign of her crew, who had mysteriously disappeared without a trace. Where had they gone? And why had they deserted a ship that was far from sinking?

The most likely explanation is that the crew had fled in panic. But what had happened to scare them? And were the unidentified bodies found on a raft early the next year all that remained of the doomed *Mary Celeste* crew?

Do you believe in fairies? Elsie Wright and her cousin Frances Griffiths said they did. In fact, they even found some living at the bottom of Elsie's garden. And to prove it, they took some amazing pictures

During the hot summer of 1917, Frances and Elsie took five photographs that stunned the world.

They showed the girls playing with their friends near a brook in Cottingley, West Yorkshire. Nothing unusual about that, you might think – except these friends turned out to be fairies!

READ ALL ABOUT IT!

Lots of other people believed in the fairies too – including Sir Arthur Conan Doyle, the famous creator of Sherlock Holmes and a firm believer in the supernatural. Conan Doyle had the photographs tested and declared that they were not fakes. He wrote about the case in *Strand* magazine, complete with "the most astounding photographs ever published". It sold out in days and caused a huge stir all over the country.

CLOSE ENCOUNTERS

Years later, Elsie and Frances admitted that the 'fairies' were paper cut-outs, propped up by hat pins and brooches. Frances said they had faked the photographs because it had proved impossible to photograph the real fairies they had seen in the garden. But Elsie claimed they had originally planned the prank to keep Frances out of trouble for falling in a brook.

Some UFO experts claim that stories of encounters with fairies are so similar to stories of close encounters with aliens that they must be one and the same thing. Perhaps that's why Frances and Elsie thought their flighty fairy friends were out of this world!

FAIRY DIFFICULT!

Can you answer these testing fairy teasers?

1 What is the fairy called in JM Barrie's *Peter Pan*?

2 Whose famous fairy godmother told her, "You shall go to the ball!"

3 In Shakespeare's *A Midsummer Night's Dream*, who are the king and queen of the fairies (left)?

Answers overleaf

FAIRY TALES!

Are there fairies at the bottom of your garden? Capture them on camera and you could become famous!

▲ *Frances (above) and Elsie, (above left) frolic with the fairies in Cottingley, West Yorkshire*

A FUNGI TO BE WITH?

★ Rings of toadstools are known as fairy rings. According to folklore, if you put one foot in the ring you can see the fairies. If you stand with both feet in the ring, the fairies will take you prisoner. There are also tales of people who have spent what seems to have been a night watching fairies dancing in a ring, only to return home to find 50 years of their lives have passed.

INDEX

ANSWERS TO QUESTIONS ON PAGE 30

1. Tinkerbell   2. Cinderella   3. Oberon and Titania